I feel...

happy	calm	sad	angry	worried	confident

scared	surprised	disgusted	unsure	excited	embarrassed

panicked	focused	disappointed	silly	friendly	jealous

bored	muddled	tired	unwell	hungry	hot or cold

How do I say "I feel worried" in Makaton?

I feel

Take one hand with your thumb and middle finger pointing to your face and lift your hand and say, "I feel".

worried.

With a worried look on your face, tense your hand and make small circles above your forehead and say, "worried".

ISBN 978-1-78270-695-3

Copyright © Channon Gray

All rights reserved. No part of this publication may be reproduced or utilised in any form or by any means electronic or mechanical, including photocopying, recording, or by any information storage and retrieval system now known or hereafter invented, without the prior written permission of the publisher and copyright holder.

No part of this book may be used or reproduced in any manner for the purpose of training artificial intelligence technologies or systems. In accordance with Article 4(3) of the DSM Directive 2019/790, Award Publications Limited expressly reserves this work from the text and data mining exception.

First published 2026

Published by Award Publications Limited
The Old Riding School, Welbeck, Worksop, S80 3LR

awardpublications @award.books
www.awardpublications.co.uk

25-1206 1

Printed in China

All About
Worried Scribble

Written and illustrated by
Channon Gray

award

shhhhhh!

Worry is sneaky.

Uhh! I am Worried Scribble.

It can make our thoughts turn all tricky and queasy.

Worry can sometimes feel like it has come out of **nowhere!**

Other times, it comes from shining a light on worrying thoughts that can **pop up anywhere.**

Being worried feels and looks different for everyone.

It might make you want to

freeze,

fight   or take flight and run.

It is important to give our feelings, like worry, a name...

What are you feeling? I am Name-It Scribble.

I feel worried.

...so we can understand them, and not just carry on feeling the same.

Feeling worried can keep us safe from danger and stop us from getting hurt.

Worry reminds us to

pause, think

and stay

alert.

Stop, pause and breathe!
I am Stop Scribble.

Worry makes us run away from

BIG fierce tigers

and tiny cute spiders.

It helps to guard us from things that might scare or surprise us.

However, sometimes our brain gets it wrong and we feel worried when we don't need to.

It can make us feel afraid about things that just aren't true!

Feeling worried is like our brain having its very own smoke alarm.

It warns us of danger, though sometimes there's no threat of harm.

Like talking in front of our class,

being scared of making mistakes

or even feeling worried to say goodbye to our family at the school gates.

Worry likes to let us know it is there,

by making our knees wobbly and our bodies hyper-aware.

Worry can make us feel **sick,** our **breathing go faster,** our head feel **d i z z y** and our tummy fill with butterflies.

What can you spot? I am Spot-It Scribble.

Our hands get all sweaty, our legs start to **s h a k e** and our heart rate starts to **rise.**

Worries can grow quickly, like a plant,

out of control,

but focusing on the here and now should be our goal.

If it's unlikely to happen, we can take a deep breath and let go of the fear...

count to 3

breathe in

breathe out

breathe in

breathe out

Let's take a moment!
I am Breathe Scribble.

...which helps our thinking clear.

If you catch yourself worrying while at school or out and about,

don't let those niggly worries sprout or shout.

Park them until **Worry Time,**

then give them your attention.

With a trusted grown up, chat about your fears to reduce your tension.

Worry Time is when we set aside 10 minutes each day to think about our worries.

Talk them through with a grown-up to see if they're real, or just our mind's made-up stories.

Worry Time comes with rules we must follow.

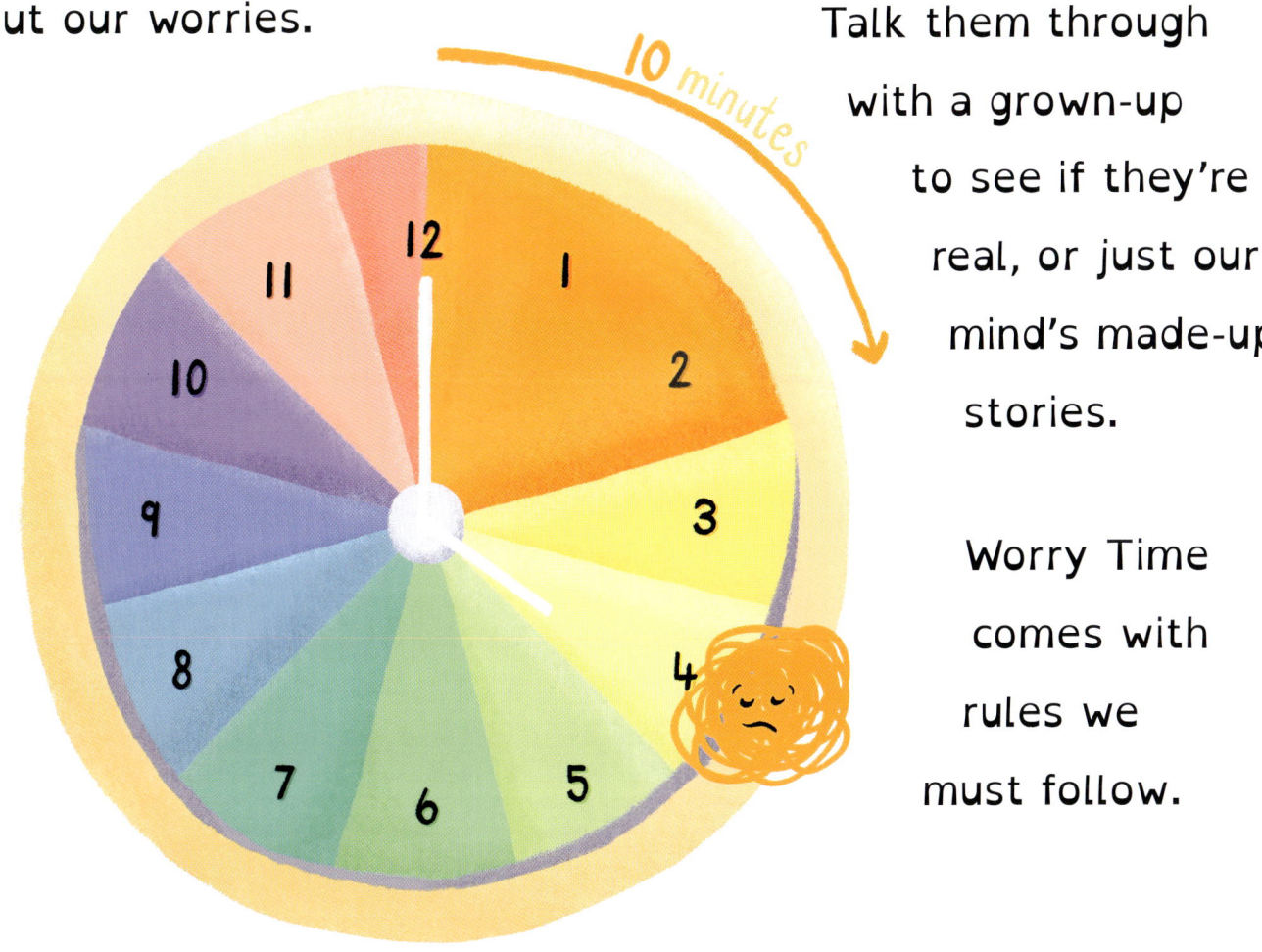

It should be in a place that feels comfortable and safe, but not near bedtime, so the worries don't trickle into tomorrow.

Feeling worried can feel so tough,

but it shows us that we're strong enough.

It's okay for worries to pop up sometimes,

like a mouse giving a squeak.

Worried Scribble Activities

Decorate an old shoebox and to make a 'Worry Box'. Write your worries on scraps of paper and post them in, ready to read at Worry Time.

Blow some bubbles. Think of each bubble as one of your worries and watch them float away and pop!

Imagine your worry as a small, funny-looking creature to make it less scary. It could be spiky or wobbly, and wear silly hats or big glasses!

The Scribbles Crew love to see your creations! Ask your grown-ups to share them on social media using #TheScribblesCrew

Scan the QR code on the back cover for more great Scribbles Crew activities, sing-along songs and teaching resources specially created by The Exciting Teacher.

www.thescribblescrew.com